W0259660

AN ADVENTURER'S GUIDE TO ANCIENT EGYPT

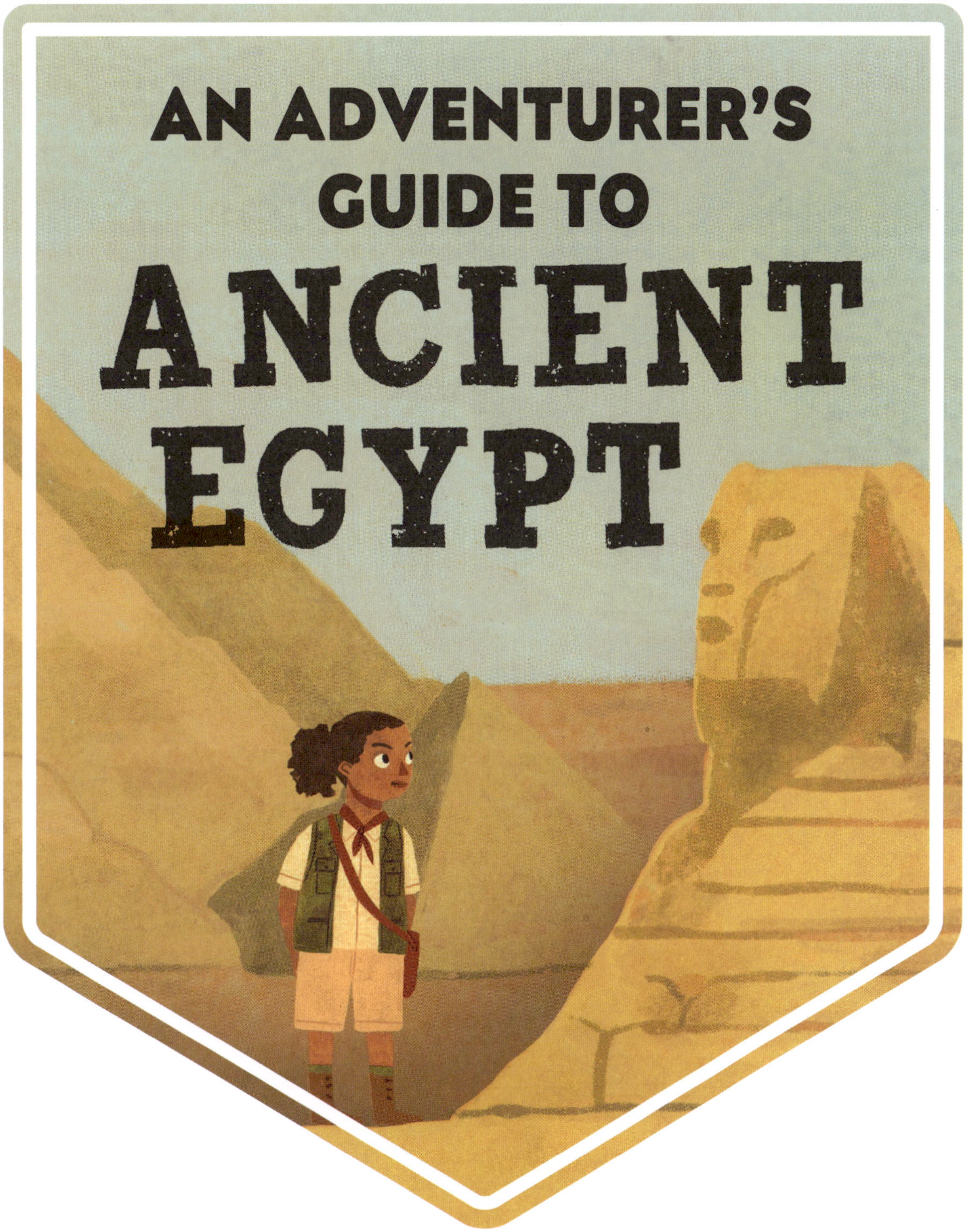

WRITTEN BY
ISABEL THOMAS

FOREWORD BY
YASMIN EL SHAZLY

ILLUSTRATED BY
YAS IMAMURA

LADYBIRD BOOKS
Ladybird Books is part of the Penguin Random House group of companies whose addresses can be found at global.penguinrandomhouse.com.
www.penguin.co.uk www.puffin.co.uk www.ladybird.co.uk

Penguin Random House UK

First published 2024
001

Text by Isabel Thomas
Illustrations by Yas Imamura
Consultant: Joyce Tyldesley
With thanks to Phoebe Farag-Mikhail

Printed in China
The authorized representative in the EEA is Penguin Random House Ireland, Morrison Chambers, 32 Nassau Street, Dublin D02 YH68
A CIP catalogue record for this book is available from the British Library
ISBN: 978–0–241–47187–6
All correspondence to:
Ladybird Books, Penguin Random House Children's
One Embassy Gardens, 8 Viaduct Gardens
London SW11 7BW

This book contains an Egyptian adventure on every spread! These interactive activities should be carried out safely with support from an adult and plenty of space to move around.

CONTENTS

BOARDING PASS

Hi, there! I'm Mia, and this is my amazing time machine. Are you ready for a new adventure?

Foreword

Ancient Egypt is a fascinating place. In fact, it is so fascinating that some people spend their entire lives studying it! These people are called Egyptologists. They study the people, buildings, language, art, objects, beliefs and history of ancient Egypt. Egyptologists can work on archaeological digs, in schools, universities, museums and more! You might even see them on television.

Egyptologists are like detectives. They collect clues about how people in ancient Egypt lived their lives, beginning from around 5,000 years ago! I am an Egyptologist and I love my job. To me, it is like an adventure to an ancient land! My "time machine" is filled with the ancient texts I read, the museums I visit and the archaeological digs I take part in. I also learn a lot from all the wonderful books that have been written by other Egyptologists.

This book will teach you so much about ancient Egypt. There is a lot to learn, so enjoy the ride!

Yasmin El Shazly

Museum mysteries

The amazing objects in this museum are from ancient Egypt. Today, Egypt is a bustling country that joins north-east Africa and the Middle East. Thousands of years ago, it was home to some of the very first farms, cities, governments, laws, technology and art in the world.

Objects from ancient Egypt give us clues about how people used to live long ago. They can even help us understand the way we live now. Many things we do today were also done by ancient Egyptians – such as carrying lucky objects, keeping cats and telling the time!

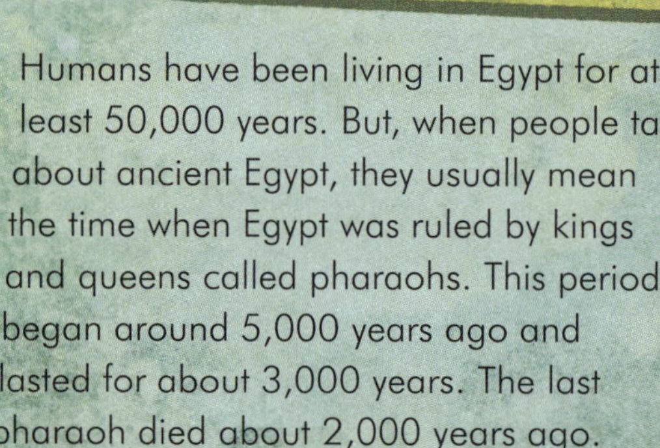

Humans have been living in Egypt for at least 50,000 years. But, when people tal about ancient Egypt, they usually mean the time when Egypt was ruled by kings and queens called pharaohs. This period began around 5,000 years ago and lasted for about 3,000 years. The last pharaoh died about 2,000 years ago.

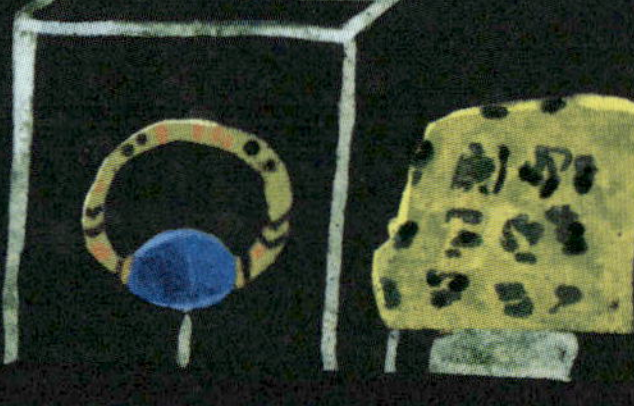

Since that time, millions of things made

Egyptian adventure

When we first look at ancient objects, we use our own lives to try and understand them. To find out how the ancient Egyptians really lived, Egyptologists look for other kinds of evidence, too.

Look at the different objects on this page. Which ones grab your attention? What do you think they were used for?

People who study ancient Egypt are called Egyptologists.

Sometimes, important clues are missing from the objects we discover. We still have many questions about ancient Egypt, and Egyptologists are using science to find answers in exciting new ways.

The Nile River

Egypt has very hot and dry weather throughout the year. It hardly ever rains, so most of the country is desert. One of the longest rivers in the world runs through these desert lands. Today, this river is known as the Nile. It was a huge part of life in ancient Egypt.

For most of the 50,000 years that people have lived in Egypt, they have moved around to hunt and gather food. But, around 8,000 years ago, people began to live in villages near the Nile. They would live in the same place all year round, growing food on farms.

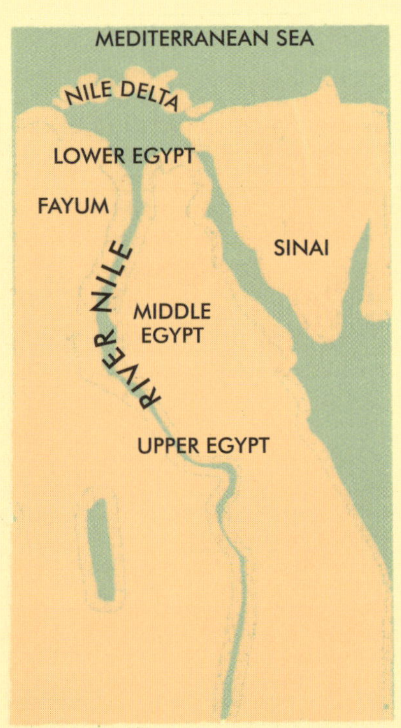

The Nile flows through Egypt to the Mediterranean Sea in the north. There are huge areas of rocky and sandy desert on both sides of the river. But the Nile River Valley is lush and green. The place where the river splits and flows into the Mediterranean Sea is called the Nile Delta.

The banks of the Nile were the perfect place to set up farms and villages. People had water to grow crops, fish to catch and mud to make bricks for building homes. They could also travel to other parts of Egypt by boat.

The Nile flooded every year, rising many metres higher than normal. The floods would spread far across the river valley. When the floodwater went down, it would leave behind layers of sand and clay, which made the land very good for growing crops like wheat.

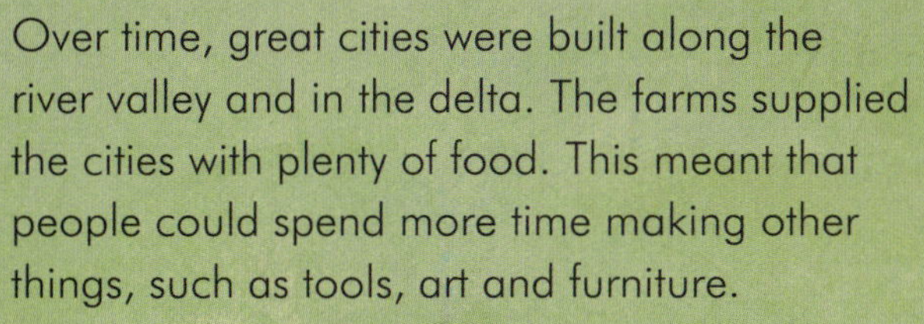

Over time, great cities were built along the river valley and in the delta. The farms supplied the cities with plenty of food. This meant that people could spend more time making other things, such as tools, art and furniture.

Egyptian adventure

A lot of ancient Egyptian pottery was decorated with pictures of local animals and wavy lines, which may have been paintings of the Nile River! Draw an outline of a vase, and decorate it with pictures of animals that live near you. What else would you paint? What might people in the future learn if they saw your paintings?

The ancient Egyptians made lots of items out of clay, which they collected from the banks of the Nile. In fact, most of the objects archaeologists have found in ancient Egypt are beads and pieces of pottery! They can tell us a lot about how people lived.

Pottery vases and jars were made to store water and food, as well as things like medicine and perfume.

The oldest Egyptian pottery is pink, the same colour as the desert clay.

The first pharaoh

For a long time, different areas along the Nile River were ruled by different leaders. The king who brought the two areas together is now said to be the first pharaoh of Egypt.

Historians think that the first pharaoh was a man called Narmer. By bringing Lower Egypt and Upper Egypt together, Narmer made Egypt one of the richest and most powerful parts of the world.

Narmer probably became the first pharaoh by winning battles against people living in other areas of Egypt. From then on, Narmer would have collected a share of the crops, farm animals and workers from all along the Nile, making him rich and powerful.

For 3,000 years, keeping both areas of Egypt together was part of each pharaoh's role. The pharaohs wore a double crown – one crown for Upper Egypt and one crown for Lower Egypt. This showed that they ruled over both areas of Egypt.

Egyptian adventure

Look at the cover of this book. The most important pictures and writing are the biggest, because we want you to look at them first! The artists from ancient Egypt used the same trick. They changed the sizes of people, animals and objects in pictures to show how important they were.

We know about Narmer because of carvings like the ones on this stone. The stone is decorated with carvings that celebrate Narmer's power.

The carvings on this stone give us lots of clues that Narmer was the first pharaoh. The first clue is his size! Pharaohs were often carved much bigger than other people, in order to show their power.

The second clue is in these two fierce-looking long-necked beasts. Many objects from ancient Egypt have pictures like this. The beasts are like Upper and Lower Egypt – they are being held together.

Learning to write

The ancient Egyptians were some of the first people in the world to invent ways of writing down information. They invented different kinds of writing. The most famous is a type of picture writing called hieroglyphs.

As towns and cities grew bigger, life in ancient Egypt became busier and more complicated. Pharaohs and their officials had to collect taxes, plan large projects and make sure farms were being run properly. They needed a way to record large numbers and lots of names.

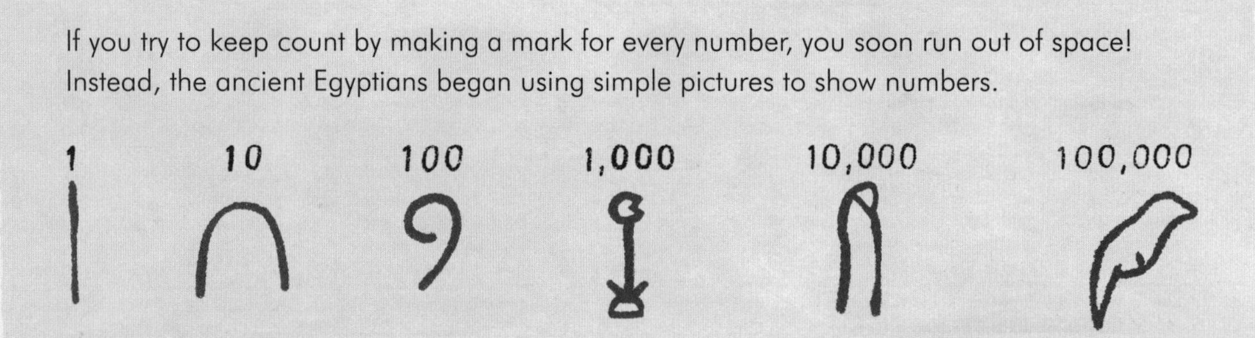

These simple pictures are called hieroglyphs. They were also used to write words. Sometimes a single hieroglyph was used to write a whole word. Sometimes, one hieroglyph was used for each sound in the word – just like the letters in our alphabet.

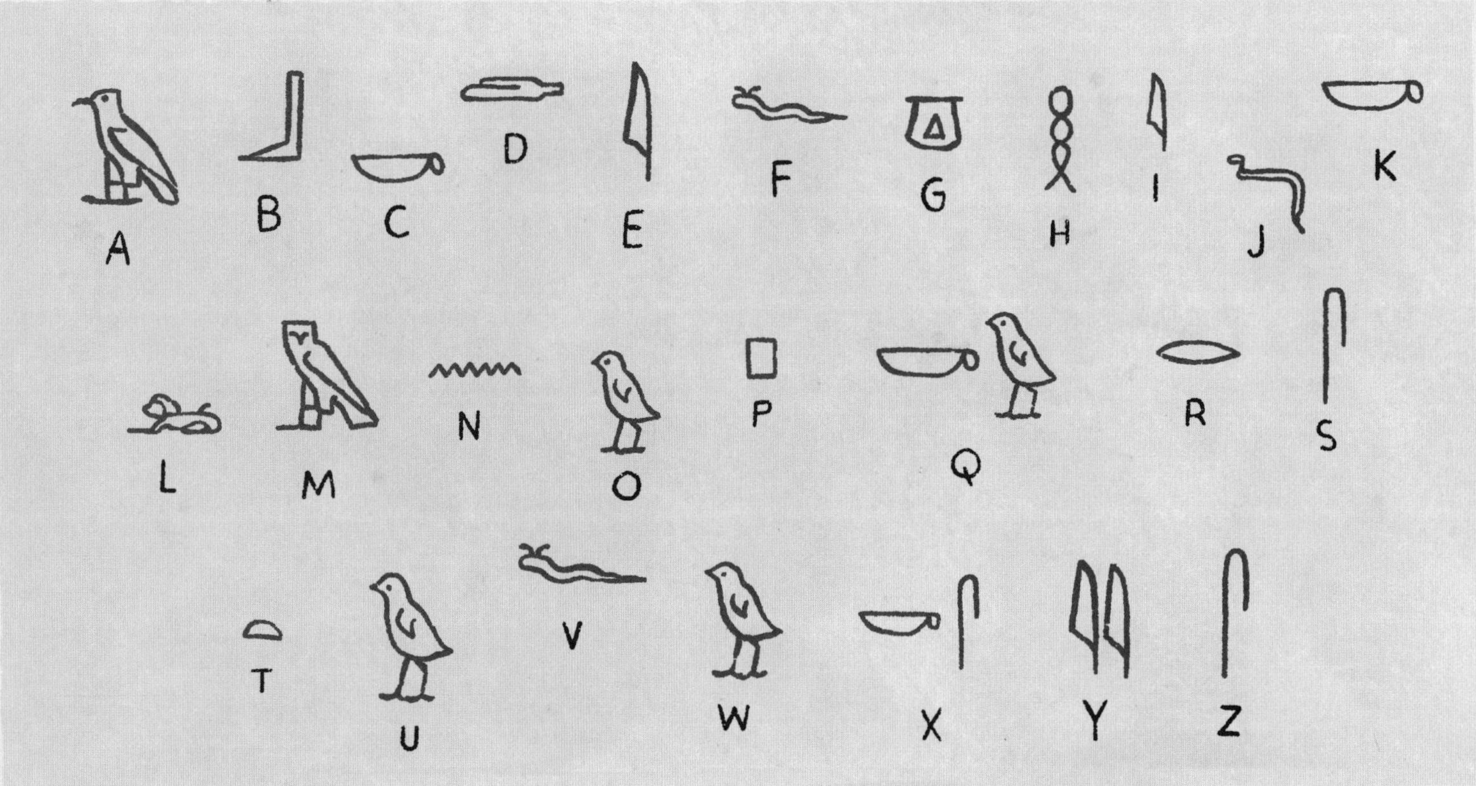

Altogether, the ancient Egyptians invented more than 7,000 different hieroglyphs.

Egyptian adventure

Try spelling your name using hieroglyphs, like Mia! The special alphabet on page 12 will help you. Just as in ancient Egypt, each picture stands for an object, but also a sound. For example, a hand stands for the sound "d". If a sound from your name is missing, try inventing your own picture for it.

Over thousands of years, the ancient Egyptians developed simpler ways to write down their language, but they kept using hieroglyphs to decorate tombs and temples, and to keep a record of important events.

This scribe is showing me how to write my name using hieroglyphs!

Making papyrus

The ancient Egyptians invented a type of paper to write on, called papyrus. It was made from the papyrus reeds that grew in the swampy Nile Delta.

To make sheets of papyrus, workers peeled off the tough outer layers to reach the soft, spongy pith in the middle of the reeds. They laid out thin strips of pith side by side in two layers, then pressed them together and dried them in the sun. As the layers dried, they glued together as one smooth sheet, which was good to write on and easy to roll up.

The ancient Egyptians painted on papyrus with brushes, which they made by chewing on the tips of papyrus reeds! They also made pens from these reeds.

Black ink was made from soot, and coloured paints were made by grinding up different coloured rocks.

Ancient Egyptians would join together up to 20 pieces of papyrus to make long scrolls. A scroll was the ancient Egyptian version of a book.

Egyptian adventure

The paper we use today is also made from plants. Take a very close look at the paper used to make this page. Can you see the tiny fibres that have been pressed together into a thin layer?

The ancient Egyptians wrote on many other materials, too. They stamped writing into bricks. They carved hieroglyphs into stone slabs and walls. They painted words on ceilings, coffins and pottery. These materials last for a lot longer than papyrus. Egyptologists have so much ancient Egyptian writing to read!

Like us, the ancient Egyptians wrote all kinds of things, from official records and letters, to stories, poems and songs. However, not everyone in Egypt could read and write – only rich people, officials and specially trained scribes.

So, although we have lots of writing from ancient Egypt, it cannot always tell us about the lives of ordinary people, because they were not usually able to write their experiences down.

The hieroglyph for "thinking" and "knowing" was a picture of a rolled-up scroll.

Gods and goddesses

The ancient Egyptians believed in many different gods and goddesses, and they worked hard to please them. People believed that keeping the gods happy would bring good luck in this life and an afterlife.

Over 3,000 years, the ancient Egyptians worshipped hundreds of different gods and goddesses.

Each local area had its own temples, each one built in honour of a god or goddess. Lots of people worked in these temples and in the buildings around them, carrying out special rituals to honour the gods.

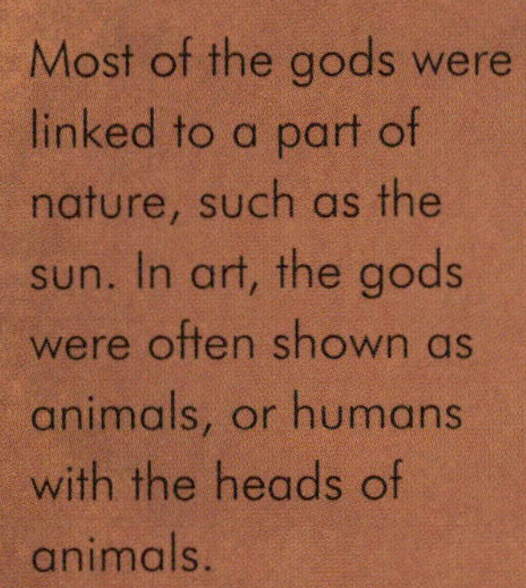

Most of the gods were linked to a part of nature, such as the sun. In art, the gods were often shown as animals, or humans with the heads of animals.

People left all kinds of gifts, or offerings, to the gods. Offerings included everyday objects like loaves of bread, but also treasures such as copper, bronze and gold statues.

Thoth was the god of the moon and wisdom. Ancient Egyptians believed that he weighed a person's heart after they died, to decide whether they could continue to the afterlife.

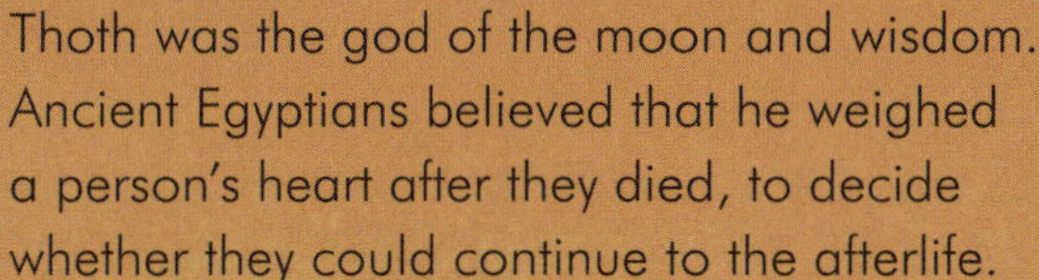

Osiris was the god of the dead and the underworld. But he was also celebrated for beginning new life, by bringing the Nile floods. He is shown like a human, but with a green face and hands.

Isis was the goddess of healing and magic, and she was the wife of Osiris. She brought Osiris back to life after he was killed by his brother, Seth.

Horus was the son of Isis and Osiris. He was a god of the sky and of kings. He was shown with the head of a hawk.

The ancient Egyptians told exciting stories about the gods and goddesses. In these myths, some of the gods were members of the same family.

The ancient Egyptians believed in the gods and their powers. At that time, people did not know the scientific reasons why the Nile flooded every year, why the sun rose and set in the sky, or what caused different illnesses. Instead, they explained these events with stories about the gods.

Egyptian adventure

Egyptologists are puzzled about what kind of animal Osiris's brother, Seth, was! In art and statues, he has a long snout and long ears with square tips. Sometimes, he has a tail with a tuft. Ask an adult to help you find a picture of Seth in a book or online. What kind of animal do you think he was?

The first pyramid

The pharaohs were thought of as half god, half human. After they died, they became gods. To prepare for this, each pharaoh built giant temples and tombs. The most famous of these are the pyramids.

More than 100 ancient Egyptian pyramids are still standing. The oldest was built by a pharaoh called Djoser.

The Pyramid of Djoser is made of limestone blocks piled 62 metres high. It looks like a giant staircase, so it's also known as the Step Pyramid.

Djoser built this pyramid as his tomb – he planned to be buried there after he died.

The Step Pyramid was designed by an architect called Imhotep. He became so famous that, hundreds of years later, the ancient Egyptians began to think of him as a god.

Lots of objects were placed inside each tomb, to help the dead person in the afterlife. These included food, everyday objects like pots, treasures made from gold and precious stones, useful pieces of writing, and lucky objects called amulets. Stories about the dead person's life were painted and carved on to the walls.

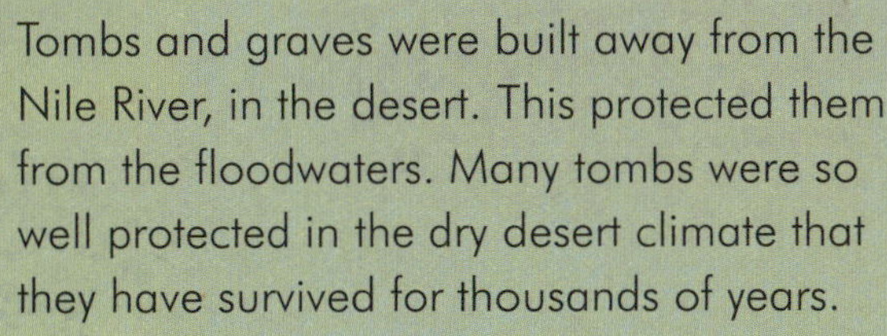

Tombs and graves were built away from the Nile River, in the desert. This protected them from the floodwaters. Many tombs were so well protected in the dry desert climate that they have survived for thousands of years.

Egyptian adventure

Close this book and try standing it upright on one edge. Is it stable or easy to knock over? Then, open it up to make a triangular structure with a wide base and a narrow top. Is it more stable? The shape of the pyramids has helped them to stay standing for nearly 5,000 years. The way they were built has also helped – the stones were cut and fitted together very carefully.

There are miles of tunnels, shafts and corridors underneath the Step Pyramid.

Tombs – and the objects inside them – have survived far longer than ancient Egyptian villages, towns and cities. They are one of the main ways we find out how people lived in ancient Egypt.

This explains why so many ancient Egyptian objects in museums today came from tombs!

The pharaohs worked hard to show that they were keeping the gods happy. When a pharaoh won a battle, held a festival or built a monument to a god, it was as if they were bringing good luck to the whole country. These beliefs helped the pharaohs stay in power without large armies or a police force.

The Great Pyramid

After Djoser built his pyramid tomb, many other rulers copied the idea and built even better pyramids. The biggest was the Great Pyramid of Giza, built by a pharaoh called Khufu.

The Great Pyramid covers an area the size of two football pitches and was 146 metres high when built. That's almost tall enough to count as a skyscraper today! It was built thousands of years before steam power or electricity were invented.

Even with today's machines and tools, it would be a huge challenge to cut 2.3 million stones and move them into place. At the time, the only sources of power were animals and people, helped by simple ramps and pulleys!

Egyptologists worked out how the Great Pyramid was built by combining historical evidence and science. An ancient wall painting shows a colossal statue being pulled across the desert on a sledge. In the painting, someone is pouring water on to planks in the sand.

Scientists tried this out, and discovered that using just the right amount of water helped a heavy sledge slide along more easily.

Archaeologists estimate that at least 10,000 workers would have been needed. It was another 3,800 years before anyone managed to build a taller monument!

Egyptian adventure

Close this book and lay it on a rough surface such as grass. Is it easy to push or pull along? Next, try moving it on a firmer, smoother surface. Is it easier or harder? Creating tracks in the desert sand may have helped the ancient Egyptians move stone blocks weighing 15 tonnes each from desert quarries to the places where the pyramids were built.

Khufu also built three smaller pyramids, for other members of his family.

These pyramids were built with steps, like Djoser's, but they were filled in, to make smooth sides.

Let's get out of here before we get roped in to help – it looks like hard work!

A huge tomb was a sign of the pharaoh's power. Long after the pharaoh had died, people would visit to make offerings and celebrate the pharaoh's life. In a way, this did give the pharaohs a kind of life after death.

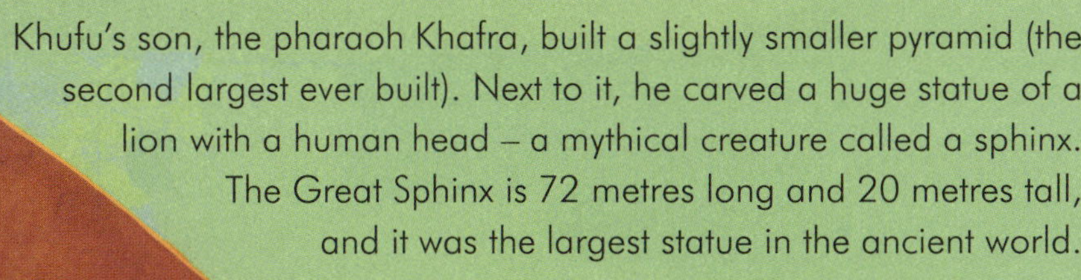

Khufu's son, the pharaoh Khafra, built a slightly smaller pyramid (the second largest ever built). Next to it, he carved a huge statue of a lion with a human head – a mythical creature called a sphinx. The Great Sphinx is 72 metres long and 20 metres tall, and it was the largest statue in the ancient world.

Making mummies

The ancient Egyptians believed that when people died they would still need their bodies in the afterlife. So, before they buried someone, they would protect the body by turning it into a "mummy".

The idea of protecting dead people's bodies like this may have come from myths about the ancient Egyptian gods, Osiris, Isis and Anubis. Anubis was a god of funerals and was shown with the head of a jackal. He was said to have wrapped up Osiris's body ready to be buried. Osiris became one of the most important gods in ancient Egypt.

People believed that things such as mummification would give a person everything they needed to gain eternal life. At first, only the bodies of powerful and rich people were mummified, but gradually more people could have their body mummified after death.

Mummification took about two and a half months.

1. The body was washed in water from the Nile.
2. Soft, squishy organs like the liver, lungs, stomach and intestines were removed, and stored in special stone or pottery jars. These jars were buried along with the mummy.
3. The brain was removed through the nostrils. The ancient Egyptians didn't think brains were very important, so they weren't buried with mummies. The heart was left inside the body, because the ancient Egyptians believed it gave a person their personality and intelligence.
4. The body was covered with a type of salt called natron. This drew all the water out. The microbes that normally cause dead things to decay cannot survive without water.
5. The body was covered in plant oils, pine resin and other natural chemicals that stop microbes from growing.
6. Finally, the body was wrapped in long strips of linen fabric with good-luck charms called amulets. It was then placed inside a coffin within other coffins.

Mummification helped the Egyptians discover more about the human body. Studying mummies also helps today's scientists find out more about ancient Egyptians!

Coffins were decorated with pictures and hieroglyphs. These included words that were thought to be powerful.

Egyptian adventure

Mummies were often buried with amulets. They include a serpent's head, a beetle, a pillar, an eye and two frogs. See if you can spot all eight amulets hidden on this page!

Animals in ancient Egypt

Archaeologists have found hundreds of thousands of animal mummies in special animal tombs, as well as lots of statues and artworks featuring animals. These are clues that animals were important in ancient Egypt.

The ancient Egyptians kept farm animals such as goats and cattle. They used oxen to pull ploughs to plant crops, and donkeys to help carry things. They also hunted animals that lived in and near the Nile River, such as waterbirds, hippos and crocodiles.

The ancient Egyptians lived alongside cats, like me and my pet cat! But Egyptologists don't know for certain if they treated cats like pets. Read the clues on this page and see what you think.

Millions more animal mummies have been found in hidden tombs, including waterbirds, falcons, crocodiles, snakes and baboons.

Animals were important symbols. A symbol is something that has another meaning. Animals such as hawks, cats and jackals were linked to ancient Egyptian gods and goddesses.

Pharaohs were sometimes drawn with the body of an animal, to show their link with gods and goddesses. They were also linked with mighty animals such as bulls.

Egyptian adventure

Mummies of all these animals have been found in ancient Egyptian tombs. Look at the animal mummies on this page. Can you match them to the animals below?

Bastet was a cat goddess. Sometimes she was shown with the head of a lion. Mostly, she was shown as a smaller, tame cat.

In one book about ancient Egypt, an ancient Greek author reported that people would shave off their eyebrows if a cat died in their home, in order to show their grief.

The cobra was an important symbol of royalty. It was worn by the pharaoh on their forehead.

Like many people at that time, the ancient Egyptians hunted wild animals for sport. The pharaoh Amenhotep III boasted about killing more than a hundred lions.

Tracking time

The ancient Egyptians looked closely at the movements of the sun, moon and stars, spotted patterns and used them to help daily life run more smoothly.

Life in ancient Egypt was organized around the flooding of the Nile, which happened at a similar time each year.

Ancient Egyptian astronomers noticed that the star Sirius was hidden for 70 days each year, then appeared in the same place in the sky – just before the river began to rise.

By watching the movements of the stars, they could work out when the Nile was about to flood. They made some of the world's first calendars to help them plant and harvest crops at the right times, and to fix the dates of important festivals.

The ancient Egyptian calendar was based on the Nile and the stars. It had 365 days, just like our calendars today, but in other ways it was not like ours. The year count started again with each new ruler!

Egyptian adventure

Work like an ancient Egyptian astronomer. On a dark, starry night, look out of your window and pick a star in the sky. Open this book a little and place it on a hard surface, so the top of the spine is just below the star you picked. Check the star from time to time. Does it stay in the same place, or does it seem to move in the sky?

Answer: Today, we know that it's actually Earth that's moving, not the stars!

The floods made the soil wet and fertile enough to grow crops!

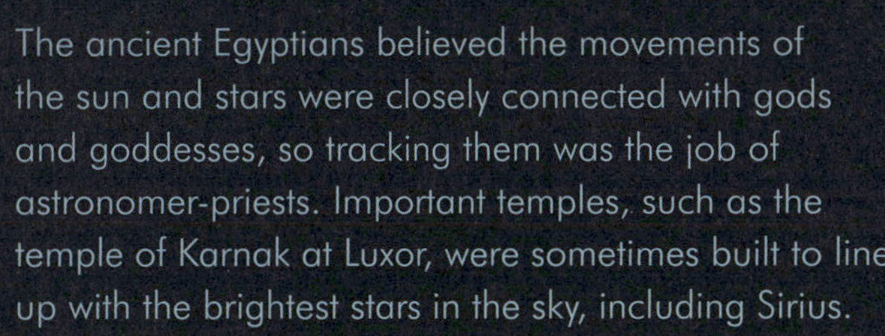

The ancient Egyptians believed the movements of the sun and stars were closely connected with gods and goddesses, so tracking them was the job of astronomer-priests. Important temples, such as the temple of Karnak at Luxor, were sometimes built to line up with the brightest stars in the sky, including Sirius.

Towering obelisks

The sun was very important to ancient Egyptians. Pharaohs carved tall monuments called obelisks to honour sun gods.

Obelisks were made when the pharaoh Hatshepsut was in charge. First, she had the obelisks cut out of rock, in one piece. This took seven months. Then, the giant stone pillars were sent down the Nile on barges pulled by 27 ships, each one rowed by hundreds of people. Finally, they were heaved into place using ropes and ramps.

The obelisks were 30 metres tall, and one is still standing today! Many other obelisks were taken from Egypt and placed in other parts of the world.

Each obelisk was polished until the stone shone. They were often covered in gold, too!

When the sun is high in the sky, the desert feels as hot as an oven! Luckily, I've landed in the shade.

There were many sun gods, but the most important was Re. He was said to bring light and life. People believed Re sailed across the sky in a boat each day, just as the sun seems to move across the sky. Many pharaohs claimed to have a very strong connection with Re.

Egyptian adventure

Stand this book up on one end on a sunny day, on a flat area of ground. Mark where the shadow falls (use chalk or stones). Leave the book where it is and come back and make a new mark every hour. Mark the time, too. The next day, you can place the book in the same position and use the shadows to tell the time, just like an ancient Egyptian!

The ancient Egyptians noticed that the shadows of objects change as the sun moves across the sky, so they used obelisks as shadow clocks to tell the time. They made smaller shadow clocks, too. Changes in shadows and stars were used to divide the day and night into 24 parts. These were a bit like our hours, but daytime hours were longer in summer and shorter in winter.

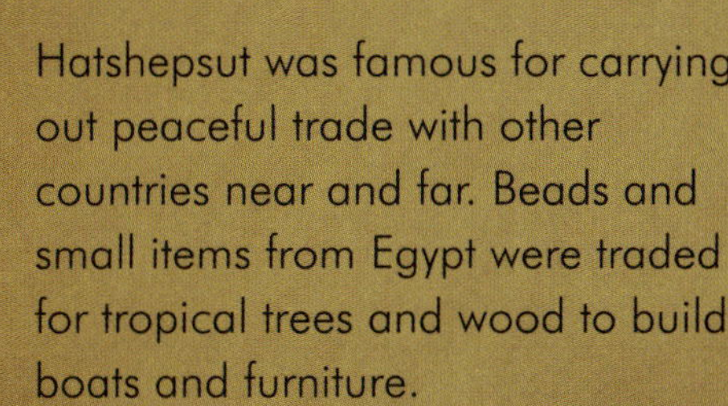

Hatshepsut was famous for carrying out peaceful trade with other countries near and far. Beads and small items from Egypt were traded for tropical trees and wood to build boats and furniture.

Hatshepsut built many grand buildings when she was pharaoh, including her mortuary temple on the west of the Nile, where the sun set every day. The temple was built into cliffs, and the most private area of the building was cut out of the rocks. Hatshepsut was not buried in the temple, though. Instead, her tomb is nearby, in the Valley of the Kings.

Getting dressed

The ancient Egyptians were interested in fashion and trends. For thousands of years, the main fabric for making clothes was linen.

Linen was woven from the fibres of flax plants grown along the banks of the Nile. It was hard work. People had to beat the flax to get the fibres, then twist the fibres together and spin them into thread that could be woven into cloth.

Even mummies wore linen! The "bandages" they were wrapped in were often strips of old linen sheets or clothes!

Linen is hard to dye, so most clothes were the natural cream colour of linen. Richer people could afford white linen that had been bleached, or even green linen made from younger flax plants.

Men wore skirts, made of rectangles of linen.

For special occasions, wealthy men and women wore long wigs made from human hair.

Most clothing began as large, simple pieces of cloth. They were styled in different ways by draping, pinning, tying and even pleating the fabric.

In most paintings, statues and other artworks, ancient Egyptians are shown with bare feet. We do not know if this was just the style for art, or if ancient Egyptians went barefoot most of the time. They knew how to make sandals out of papyrus.

Wealthy people wore huge pieces of jewellery to show off how rich and important they were. The pharaohs and their families wore the most elaborate jewellery, including huge collars and headpieces made from precious metals and gemstones.

Linen was also used to make bedding, furniture, ropes, fishing lines and sails for boats.

Egyptian adventure

Fashion was fun in ancient Egypt, but it was also designed to help people keep cool in the hot, dry climate. Fans made from leaves or feathers were popular, too. To see how they worked, close this book and wave it gently to and fro near your face. Can you feel a cooling breeze?

Perfumes and make-up were popular with men and women. They were made from natural things like plants and ground-up rocks.

Staying healthy

Pharaoh Ramesses II lived until he was about 90 years old, but most adults in ancient Egypt only lived for around 35 years. Although the ancient Egyptians knew lots about the human body, they didn't really know what caused illnesses.

People suffered from many of the same diseases and illnesses that affect humans today. However, the ancient Egyptians didn't yet understand what caused them. They often blamed evil forces or angry gods. They believed that gods and goddesses controlled every part of life, including health.

Doctors used magical spells as well as medicines. One ancient papyrus describes a cure for headaches. It tells doctors to make a clay crocodile with grain in its mouth, then tie the crocodile to the patient's head using a strip of linen with pictures of thirteen gods painted on it. The doctor also had to say a kind of magic spell.

Yikes! I think tying a crocodile to my head would *give* me a headache!

Sometimes doctors gave patients amulets to wear. These special pictures or shapes were thought to have particular powers to help people heal or avoid disease.

Dung beetles were symbols of life. The beetles rolled large balls of dung across the ground, just like the sun seemed to roll across the sky.

Ankh (key of life) was a symbol that meant eternal life.

The *Wedjet*-eye (Eye of Horus) is a symbol of good health and protection. In ancient Egyptian myths, the right eye of the god Horus was damaged by his uncle, Seth, then healed. Wearing the eye symbolized healing and new starts.

Egyptian adventure

Look at the lucky symbols that the ancient Egyptians used. Do you have any special objects that you keep, or words that you say, for good luck?

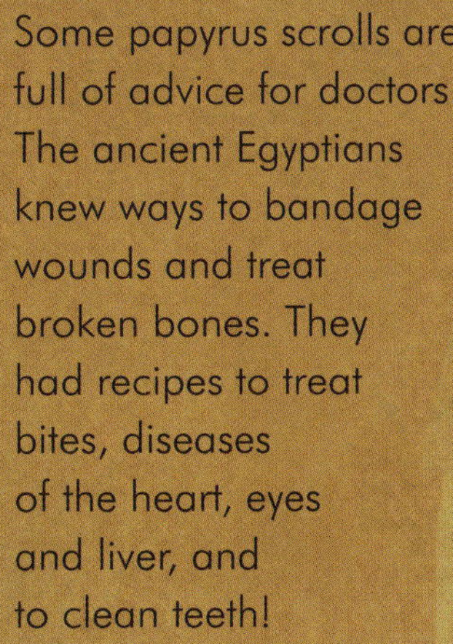

Some papyrus scrolls are full of advice for doctors. The ancient Egyptians knew ways to bandage wounds and treat broken bones. They had recipes to treat bites, diseases of the heart, eyes and liver, and to clean teeth!

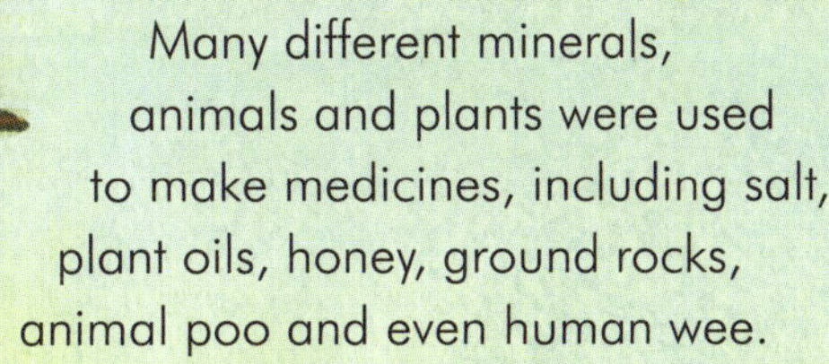

Many different minerals, animals and plants were used to make medicines, including salt, plant oils, honey, ground rocks, animal poo and even human wee.

The ancient Egyptians knew how to work with metal, so they could make copper needles and other medical tools for surgery.

The ancient Egyptians didn't have the kinds of doctors we do today. Instead, clever people did a bit of everything! The famous architect Imhotep was also a doctor, surgeon, astronomer, priest and advisor!

Many amulets were made from a special type of material called faience. Like glass, faience was mainly made of sand. Small amounts of metal were added to create bright and beautiful colours. The ingredients were ground up to make a paste, pressed into moulds, and then fired in a kiln.

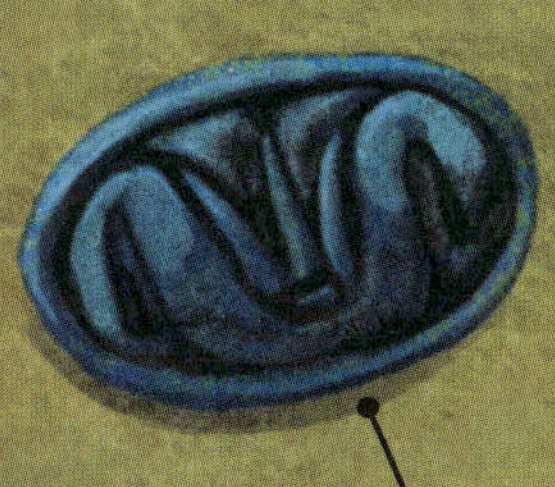

The lotus flower was a symbol of Upper Egypt and of everlasting life, because it closed at night but opened up again in the day when the sun came up.

Family life

We know lots about how rich and important people in ancient Egypt lived, because they left so many objects and records in their tombs. It is harder to find out about the lives of ordinary people, but Egyptologists are good at finding clues.

Most normal ancient Egyptian houses were made of mud bricks. This means that few have survived. For the last 2,000 years, new towns and cities have been built where ancient villages, towns and cities once stood.

Cooking was done in pottery ovens and open fires. Wheat was one of the main crops grown along the banks of the Nile River, so meals were based around bread and beer, as well as other plants such as leeks, onions, beans, lentils, melons and garlic.

The main types of meat eaten by ordinary families were fish and birds. Red meat was much more expensive and mostly eaten by richer families, as well as treats like figs, grapes and cakes sweetened with honey.

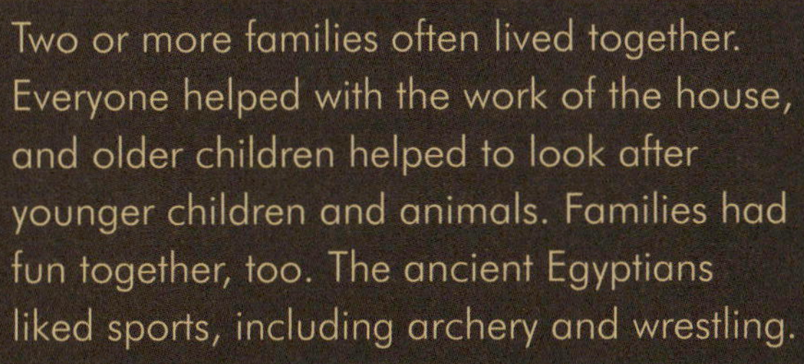

Two or more families often lived together. Everyone helped with the work of the house, and older children helped to look after younger children and animals. Families had fun together, too. The ancient Egyptians liked sports, including archery and wrestling.

Egyptian adventure

Find or make two counters, and challenge someone to a game of snake! You can use the board drawn on this page. Start at the snake's tail. Throw the dice to move your counters forward. The first to the snake's head and back again is the winner!

I'm joining the family in a game called *Mehen*. It is named after the Egyptian snake god. The round board looks like a coiled snake! Our counters look like tiny lions.

Board games were popular in ancient Egypt. Instead of using dice, people threw special sticks, or even knucklebones from a sheep or goat. The bones or sticks could land in several different ways, generating a random number.

Game boards were made of wood or even carved stone. Lots of the games were linked to the stories told about gods and goddesses.

Learning

Learning was important to ancient Egyptians. Once children were about five years old, they learned by watching and helping their parents. Some became apprentices, and trained in the same skills as their parents, like engineering, weaving, farming or sculpting.

Boys from important and wealthy families were more likely to go to lessons with people outside the family, such as priests and scribes. These lessons took place in schools that were attached to important buildings, such as the biggest temples. There, boys learned reading, writing and mathematics. Priests also taught science and medicine, and trained new priests.

I recognize this tablet from the museum! I didn't realize I was looking at someone's homework!

At writing school, boys copied out model letters and words written by their teacher. They learned important stories and sayings by heart, by copying them out again and again.

One of the most popular jobs was being a scribe. These professional writers could go into all kinds of different careers. Many boys could train to be a scribe, and it gave children from poorer families a chance to become wealthy and powerful.

Egyptian adventure

Try copying out the phrase written in hieroglyphs below, and see what it was like to have homework in ancient Egypt!

Schoolwork was done on papyrus and sometimes on tablets made from smooth, soft stone. Children could scratch writing and sums into the surface, then smooth it out and start again.

Children didn't just learn practical skills. They were taught how to live in a way that would please the gods and goddesses. This included being helpful to their parents and kind to other people.

This wax tablet is 2,000 years old, from the time when ancient Egypt was under Greek rule. It is a homework book! The child who used it was copying out a Greek saying.

Children studied important stories and sayings written down by great Egyptians of the past, such as Ptahhotep.

War and peace

For 3,000 years, ancient Egypt traded with other countries near and far. Sometimes, they battled people from neighbouring lands. At times, ancient Egypt was even ruled by other countries.

Although Egypt had lots of quarries, plants and animals, there were many things the ancient Egyptians wanted that weren't found in the Nile Valley, or in the deserts on either side. So they made links with people nearby – in Africa and Asia, and around the Mediterranean Sea.

They traded things they had lots of for materials such as silver and tin, as well as tools, exotic woods, good quality timber and perfumes.

I'm in ancient Syria, watching the Battle of Kadesh. The army of Ramesses II is fighting the Hittite army. I'm going to stay hidden!

One of the most important things the ancient Egyptians bought was lapis lazuli, a beautiful blue stone with streaks that look like gold. It came from modern-day Afghanistan, 4,000 kilometres away.

Many pharaohs were happy just to protect their own lands. Others tried to win control of other areas. They wanted to control trade routes, gather more taxes, and become even richer and more powerful.

Egyptian adventure

The agreement between Ramesses II and the Hittites is the oldest peace treaty we know about in the world. It was signed around 3,300 years ago. Today, a copy hangs in the headquarters of the United Nations in New York City, USA. It reminds us that peace is more powerful than war.

What rules do children agree to follow when they join your school? How does this help to make your school a peaceful place to learn?

Egypt was probably at its most powerful under Ramesses II. He ruled for almost 70 years and built more temples, giant statues and amazing artworks than any other Egyptian pharaoh. He built a new capital city in the north. No wonder he is remembered as Ramesses the Great!

Ramesses II became pharaoh when he was just a teenager. A part of his kingdom was attacked by a nation called the Hittites. Ramesses II was tricked into battle. He had a small army of 20,000 soldiers and 2,000 horse-drawn chariots. He was attacked by a Hittite army double the size!

When Ramesses II fought back, it was the largest chariot battle in history! Both sides claimed they won the battle, but it was more of a draw. Fifteen years later, they agreed to make peace, and even to help each other if other enemies attacked.

The last pharaohs

Around 2,700 years after the first Egyptian pharaoh came to power, ancient Egypt was invaded and taken over by the ancient Greek king Alexander the Great. Egypt became part of Alexander's huge Greek Empire.

Under Greek rule, many parts of life in Egypt carried on as normal. People came to think of Alexander as the son of the sun god Amun. He built a new capital city called Alexandria, where the Nile River met the Mediterranean Sea.

After Alexander the Great died, one of his army generals, Ptolemy, took the chance to become pharaoh. The position was passed on to Ptolemy's relatives for the next 275 years – just as it had been passed on to the relatives of ancient Egyptian pharaohs before him.

The last pharaohs were Cleopatra VII and her son Caesarion. They died just over 2,000 years ago, when the ancient Romans conquered Egypt. After that, Egypt became part of the Roman Empire.

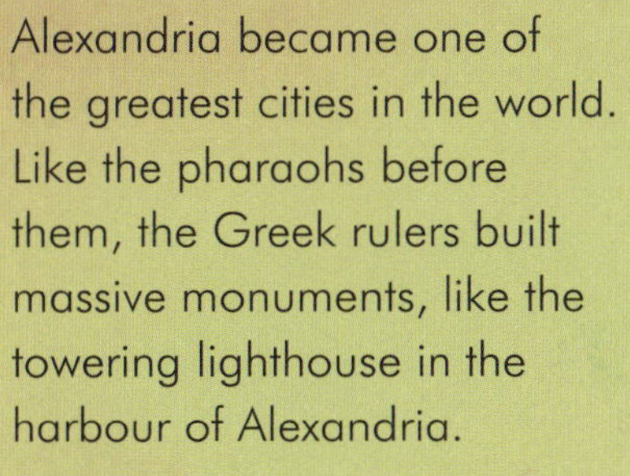

Alexandria became one of the greatest cities in the world. Like the pharaohs before them, the Greek rulers built massive monuments, like the towering lighthouse in the harbour of Alexandria.

Sadly, this lighthouse doesn't exist any more. It was destroyed by an earthquake in the Middle Ages, and a castle was built from the ruins. Cleopatra's palace was also lost below the sea during an earthquake.

The Rosetta Stone is one of the most famous objects from this time in ancient Egypt. It is a stone slab with the same message carved three times: in ancient Greek and in two types of ancient Egyptian writing. When Egyptologists first saw the stone in the early 1800s, they could finally learn how to read hieroglyphs and begin to understand what ancient Egypt was really like.

Egyptian adventure

The Rosetta Stone was first read when someone worked out that words in ovals were names. Use these names to crack the code and reveal the hidden message!

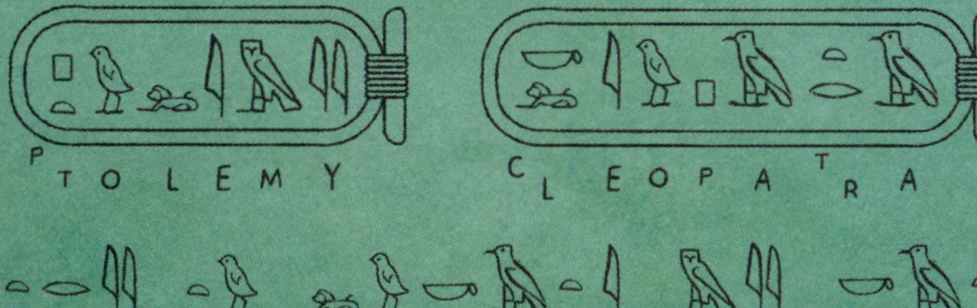

Try to locate my cat.

Egyptomania

In the 2,000 years that have passed since the last pharaohs died, many objects from ancient Egypt have been taken away to different parts of the world. But some tombs lay hidden. The most famous was the tomb of the pharaoh Tutankhamun.

After Egypt became part of the Roman Empire, the old ways of ancient Egypt slowly faded away. The people changed, integrated new religions and ways of living into their own, and found new uses for buildings and monuments.

In the 1800s, archaeologists and explorers from around the world came to Egypt to hunt for these hidden tombs and the treasures that might lie inside.

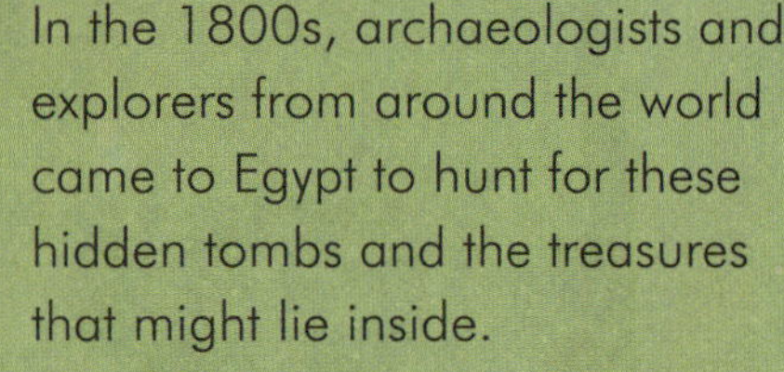

Often, archaeologists found that the tombs they discovered had been broken into long ago. The treasures that had once lain inside had been stolen and taken away. But an archaeologist called Howard Carter was certain that there was one royal tomb left to discover in the Valley of the Kings. He searched for many years.

Finally, in 1922, Howard Carter, Ahmed Gerigar, Gad Hassan, Hussein Abu Awad, Hussein Ahmed Said and their team found some hidden steps that led to an ancient doorway. Inside was the most exciting discovery – the tomb of Tutankhamun, exactly as it had been when he was buried 3,249 years earlier.

Egyptian adventure

Tutankhamun's tomb was filled with so many incredible things that it took more than ten years to remove them all. Most exciting was the mummy of Tutankhamun himself. It was covered in a solid gold death mask. Pick up this book with one hand. Tutankhamun's mask weighs as much as sixteen copies of this book!

The whole world was excited about the discovery of Tutankhamun's tomb. People wrote books and made films about ancient Egypt. Fashion designers and jewellery makers copied ancient Egyptian designs. Tutankhamun even inspired new types of music and dance. This excitement became known as "Egyptomania", and it lasted for a long time.

Egypt today

Today, we still love to discover new things about ancient Egypt, but we do this in a very different way.

We know that objects discovered by archaeologists should be left in the country where they're found, and not taken to museums far away. They belong to the people who live in that country. We can also learn much more about ancient objects if we study them in the places they are found.

Egypt has huge museums that display millions of ancient objects found in the country. The biggest museum is in the capital, Cairo. This city did not exist in ancient Egyptian times. It was built by the Arab rulers who invaded Egypt and ended Roman rule.

We are still learning new things about the ancient Egyptians – how they lived, and what they believed and thought.

Today, science and technology are an important part of an archaeologist's and Egyptologist's toolkit. Robots have been used to explore tunnels and chambers deep inside the pyramids.

Ancient Egyptian engineering was so good that many of the tombs and temples the ancient Egyptians built thousands of years ago are still standing. Millions of people visit Egypt every year to see the pyramids of Giza, the Valley of the Kings, the Karnak temple at Luxor and other famous sites for themselves.

Egyptian adventure

Ask a grown-up to help you look at a trusted news website and search for brand-new discoveries about ancient Egypt. How were they discovered? Was it by digging up ancient objects, or in a completely different way?

Thermal cameras, radio waves and laser beams have been used to scan ancient buildings and reveal hidden features. This does less damage than digging things up. We can even find out more about mummified people and animals by using X-rays and scans.

That was a fantastic trip!
Exploring the history of ancient Egypt helps us understand how people used to live long ago. It also helps us understand the way we live now. It was amazing to see the very beginning of things we take for granted today, like writing on paper and telling the time!
Archaeologists, historians, scientists and Egyptologists are still finding out new things about ancient Egypt and its peoples. Perhaps you will join their next adventure!
SOUVENIR

DINOSAURS

Glossary

afterlife	the idea of a life after death
amulet	a small object worn or carried because it is thought to bring good luck or protection
ancient	something from thousands of years ago
archaeologist	someone who finds out about the past by looking at objects and other things from that time
architect	a person who designs buildings
astronomer	a person who studies the movements of objects in space
chariot	a small vehicle with two wheels, which was pulled by horses and used in ancient times for fighting and for racing
desert	an area of land that gets very little rain or snow
Egyptologist	a person who uses science to find out about ancient Egypt
evidence	facts or information that can tell us if something is true
hieroglyphs	pictures used to represent a word, a part of a word or a sound
microbes	tiny living things that can only be seen with a microscope
mummy	the body of a human or an animal that has been preserved in a special way
museum	a building where important and interesting objects are kept and put on display
myth	a traditional story from the past that is often told, but is not thought to have really happened
obelisk	a tall stone pillar topped with a point
papyrus	a special material for writing or painting on, made from the stems of plants that are also called papyrus
pharaoh	an ancient Egyptian ruler
pottery	pots and other objects made of clay, which are shaped when wet and soft, then cooked in a hot oven to make it dry and hard
pyramid	an ancient Egyptian building with a square bottom and four triangular sides that meet at the top to form a point
ritual	a set of actions that are carried out in a certain order
scribe	a person whose job it is to write things down
temple	a special building where gods or goddesses are worshipped
tomb	a space built to bury a dead person, which can be visited to remember them

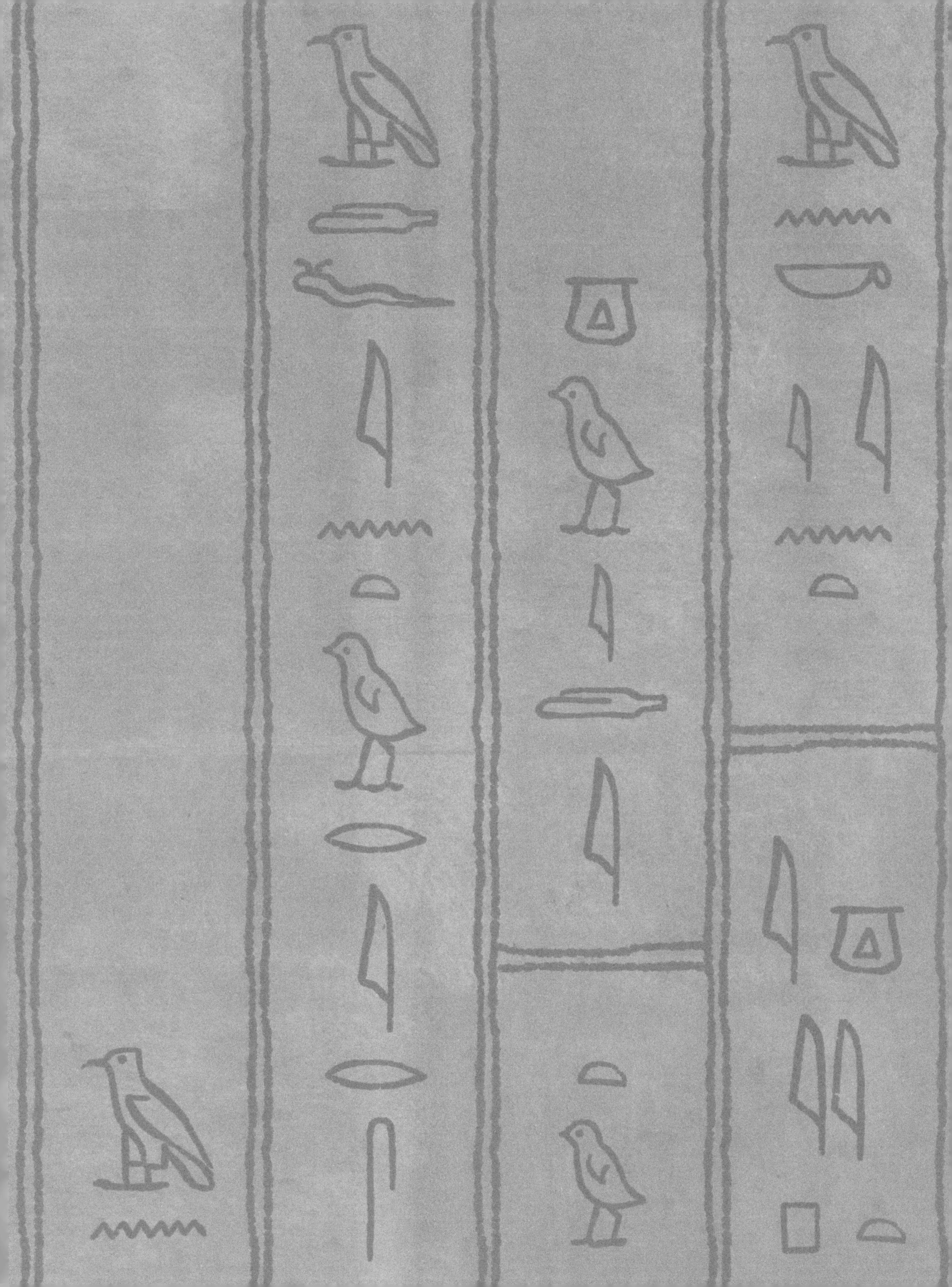